Pip's Peepers

These animals want to join in the fun too! Look out for them in every scene.

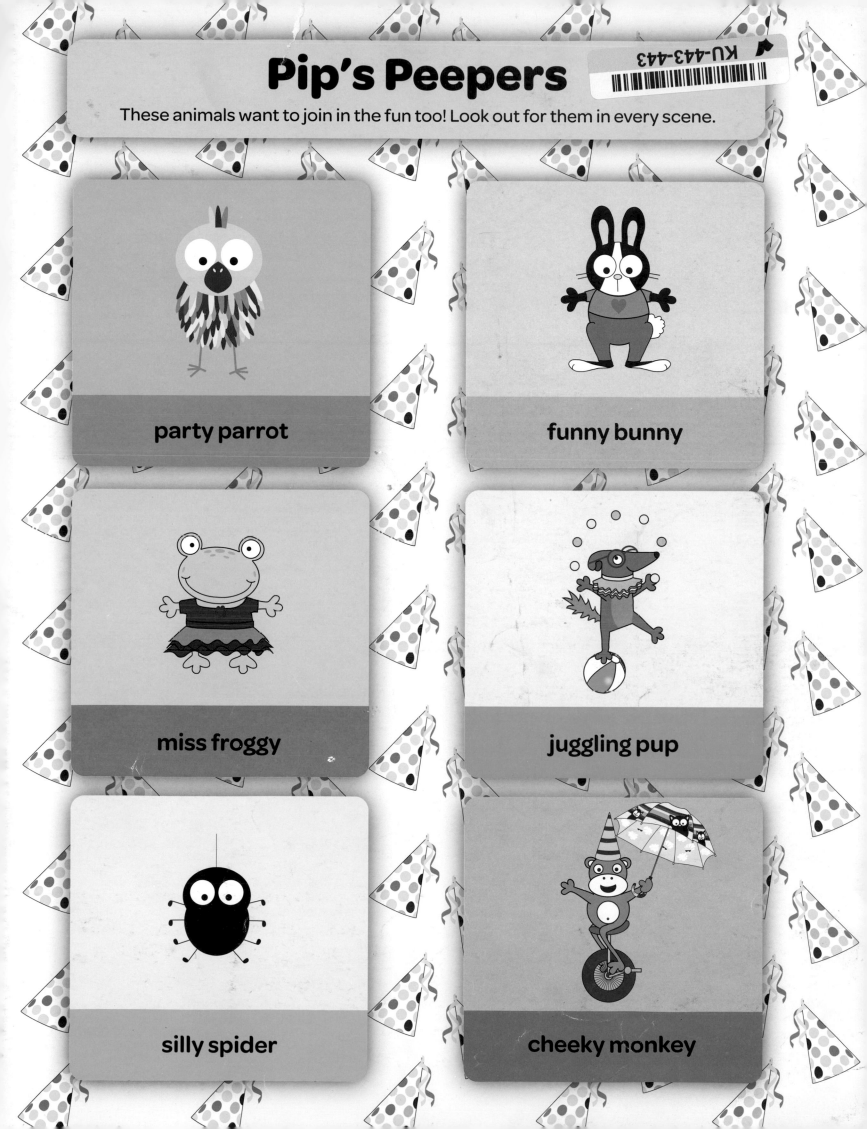

party parrot

funny bunny

miss froggy

juggling pup

silly spider

cheeky monkey

Pip's Pyjamas

Saturday night is the perfect time for a pyjama party! Everybody arrives in their cosiest nightwear. There are pillow fights, silly sleepover games and noisy hairbrush singing. Pip can't wait for the scrummy midnight feast!

Where are you Pip?

Pack up for Pip

Can you spot all of Pip's things?

We love Pip

The Valentine's ball sparkles with heart balloons,
red roses and twinkly glitter! Cool
sophisti-cats straighten their bow ties and pretty
kitties show off their fur-bulous frocks.
Pip wants to dance all night long!

Where are you Pip?

Pack up for Pip

Can you spot all of Pip's things?

Pip's Pirates and Princesses

Pip's party is packed with pussycat pirates and princesses! Some kitties dance jigs in stripy shirts. Others swish up and down in pointy pink hats. Which costume has Pip chosen today?

Where are you Pip?

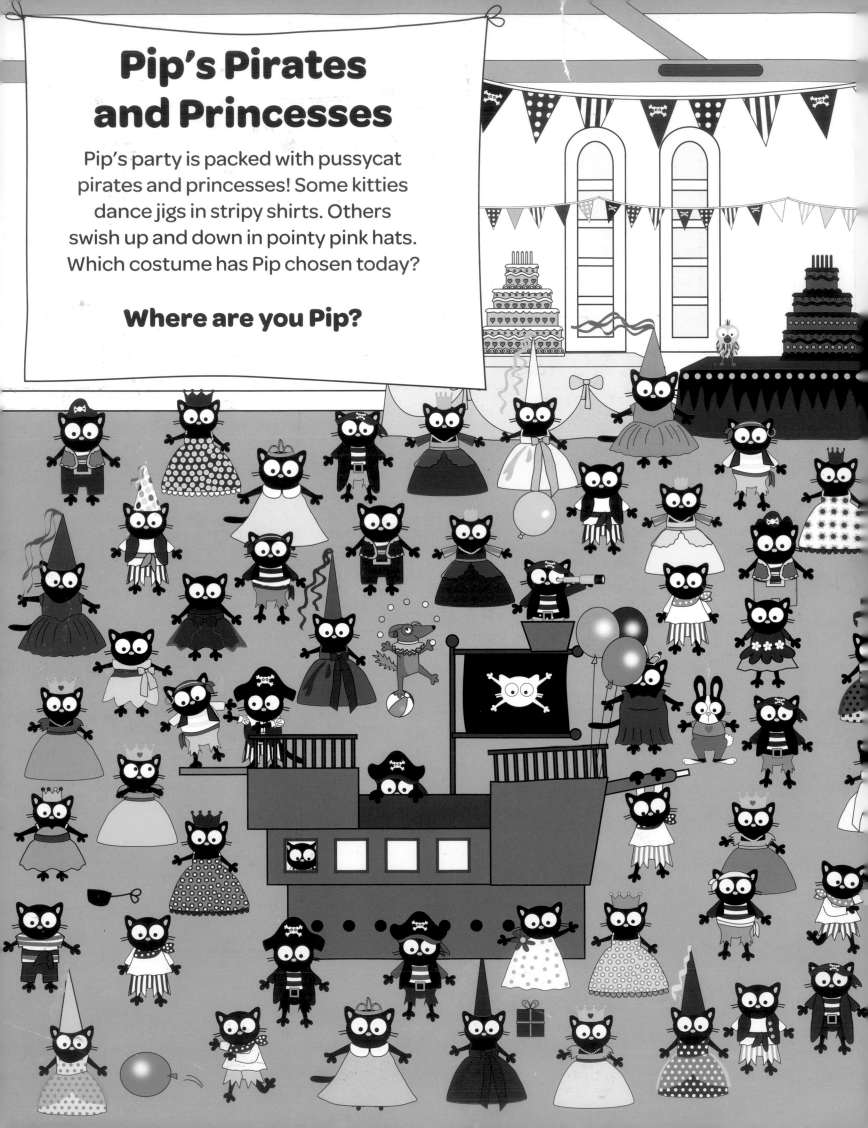

Pack up for Pip

Can you spot all of Pip's things?

Pip's Costume Cupboard

Which fancy dress do you like the best – pillaging pirates or pretty princesses?

Pip is sorting out the costume cupboard. Help the kitty put the clothes into the right piles. Draw a big, red circle around all the pirate accessories. Now draw a pink circle around the princessy pieces.

Pip's Christmas Wish

This Christmas party looks like a winter wonderland!
Skaters loop-the-loop around the ice rink while little kittens
sledge down snowy slopes.
Meow! Pip's friends are making marvellous snow-angels!

Where are you Pip?

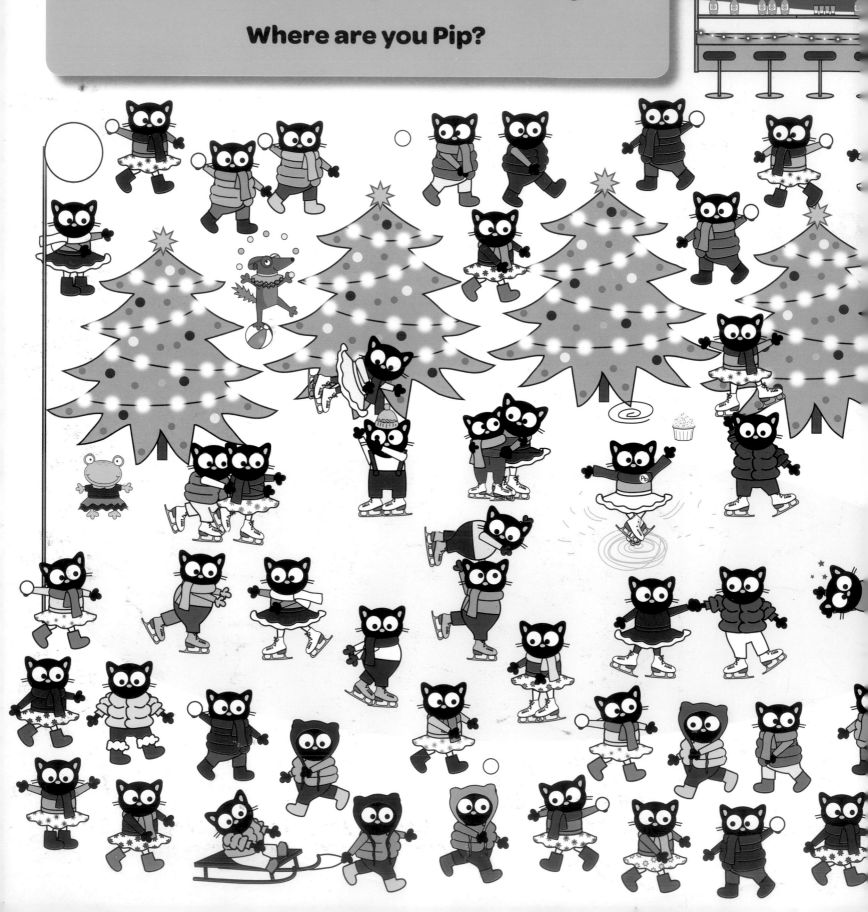

Pack up for Pip

Can you spot all of Pip's things?

Pip's Kitty Picnic

If you go down to the woods today, you're in for a big surprise!
Pip's pals are taking their teddies on a very special picnic.
Everybody sits nicely, sharing out sandwiches and cakes.
What a wonderful way to spend a sunny afternoon!

Where are you Pip?

Pack up for Pip

Can you spot all of Pip's things?

A B C D

A Path for Pip

Pip has scurried back to the house to fetch an extra rug for the teddies.
Now he can't remember which path leads back to the picnic!

Place your finger on path A, then follow it through the winding wood.
Where does it lead? Now try paths B, C and D. Which trail will take the
perplexed pussycat all the way back to the teddy bear's picnic?

Answer: B

Pip's Boogie on the Beach

The sun is out and the sky is blue for the beach barbecue of the year! Everybody grabs their coolest costumes and unrolls their towels. Soon the kitties are congaing in a funny, sunny line!

Where are you Pip?

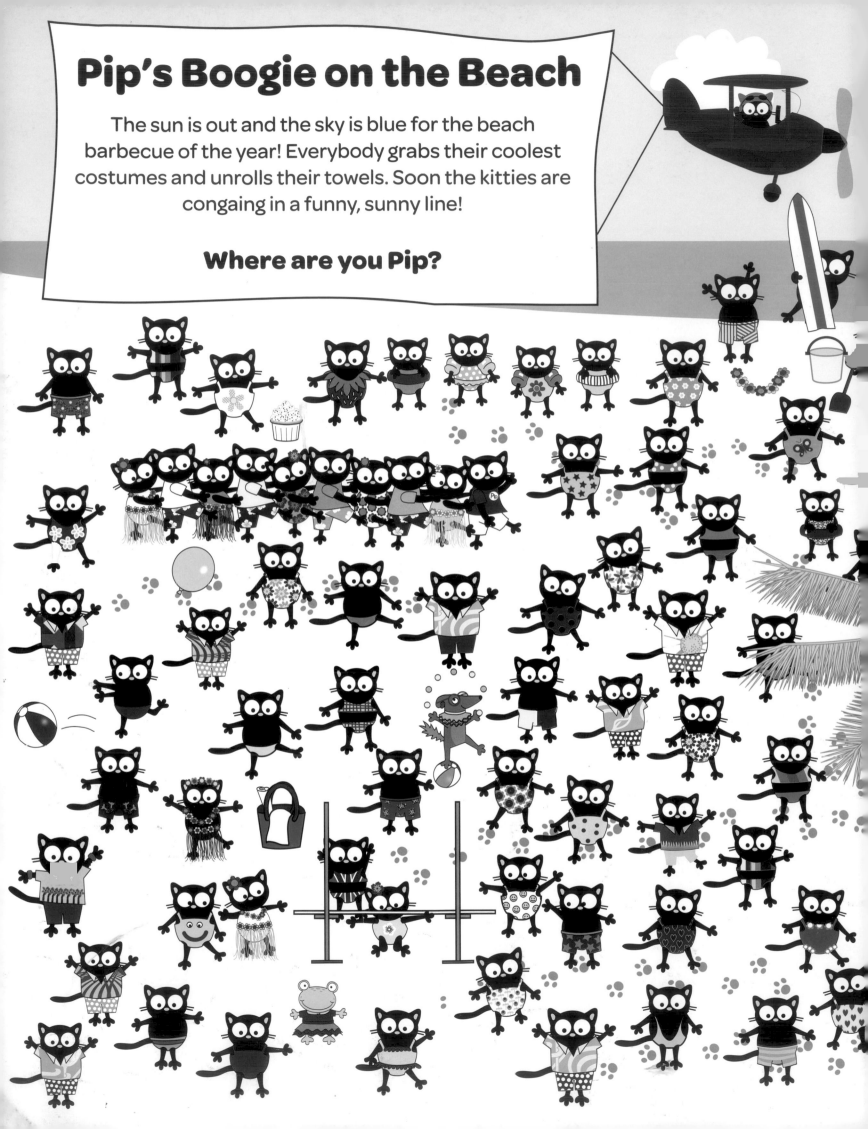

Pack up for Pip

Can you spot all of Pip's things?

Pip's Spooky Surprise

What a super, spooky party! Creepy cats in witch's hats cackle and flick their tails. It's hard to tell who is who beneath those sweeping cloaks and monster masks. Pip plays hide-and-seek amongst the pumpkin lanterns.

Where are you Pip?

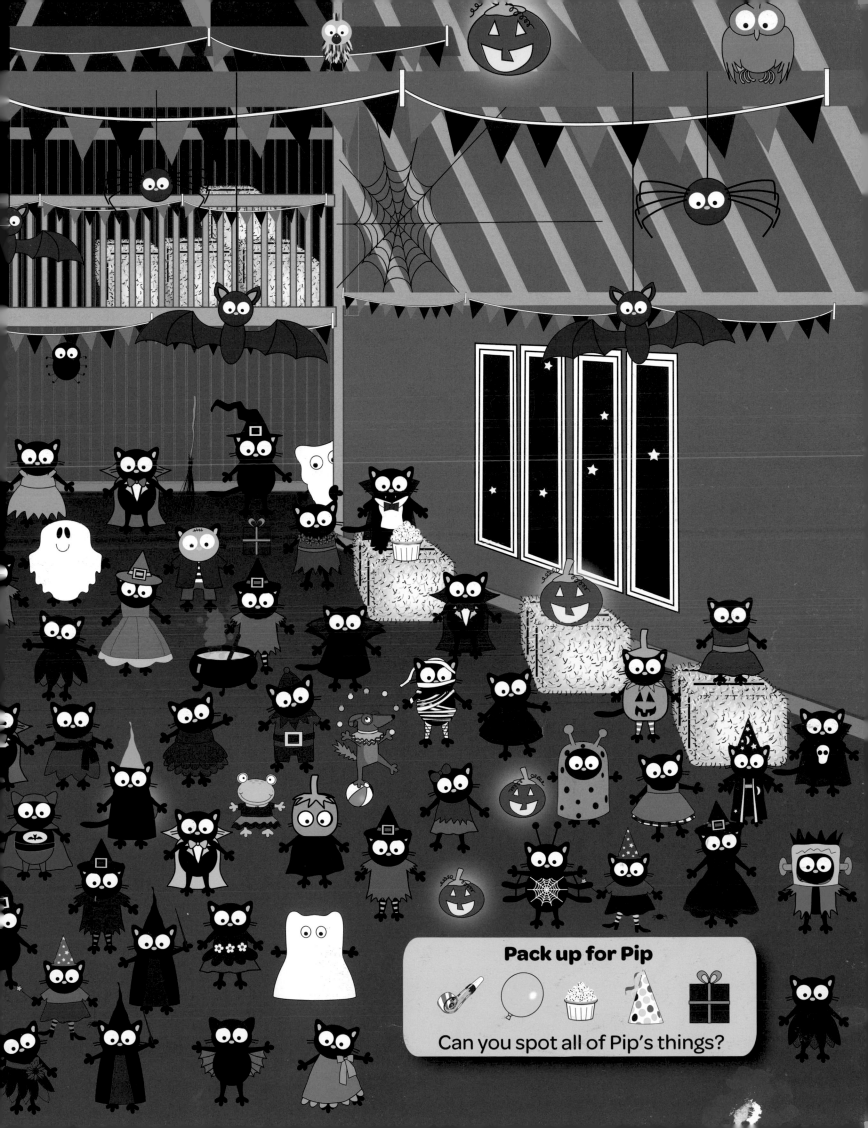

Pack up for Pip

Can you spot all of Pip's things?

Pip's Fairy Feast

Who's this tiptoeing through the flowers?
It's Pip and a garden full of fluttery, fairy friends! Every guest has chosen an enchanting costume for the magical garden party. They take it in turns to wave their wands and make sweet fairy wishes!

Where are you Pip?

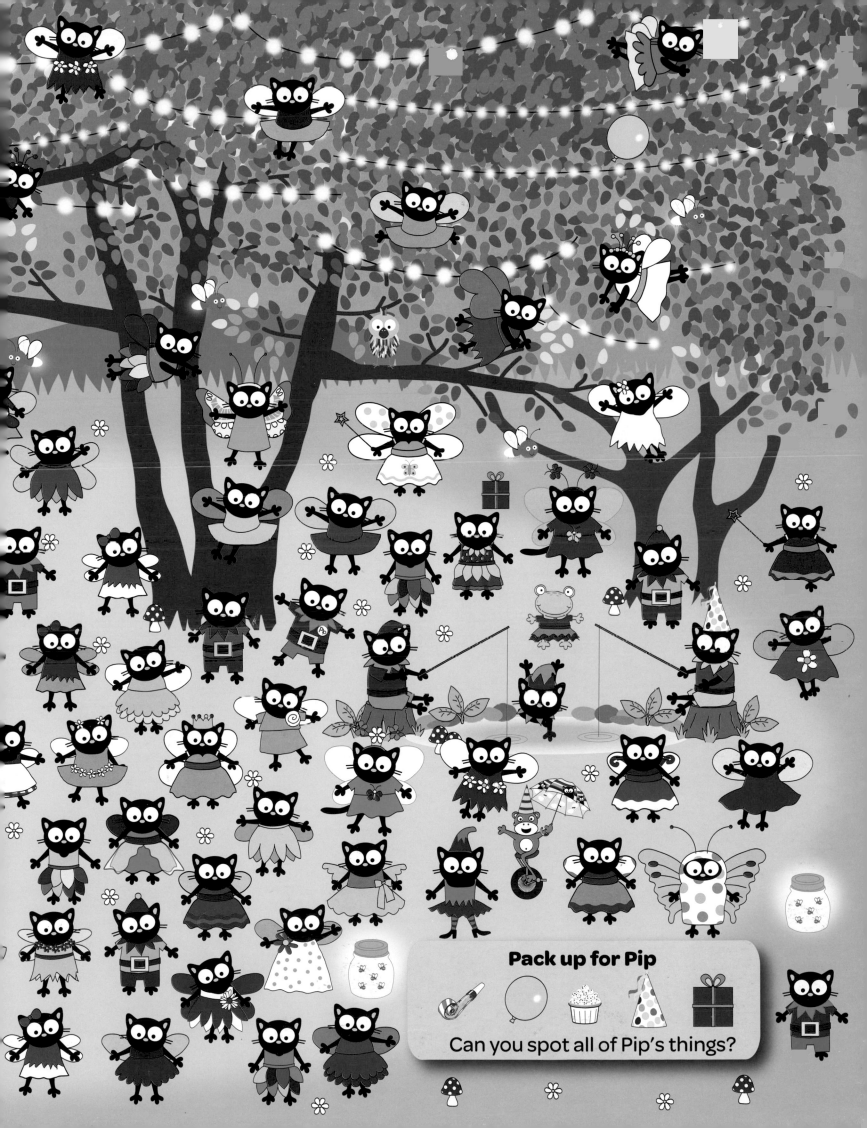

Pack up for Pip

Can you spot all of Pip's things?

Pip's Peeping Puzzle

Pip's feast sparkled with perky pixies,
beautiful butterflies and sweet fairy queens.

Look at the lines of party guests.
Can you spot the magical misfit standing in every row?
Draw a circle around the odd-kitty-out.

1. Find the fairy queen.

a **b** **c** **d** **e**

2. Pick out the pixie.

a **b** **c** **d** **e**

3. Look out for the ladybird.

a **b** **c** **d** **e**

4. Name the gnome.

a   b   c   d   e

5. Bag the butterfly.

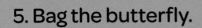

a   b   c   d   e

6. Capture the pirate captain.

a   b   c   d   e

Answers: 1B, 2D, 3C, 4E, 5D, 6A

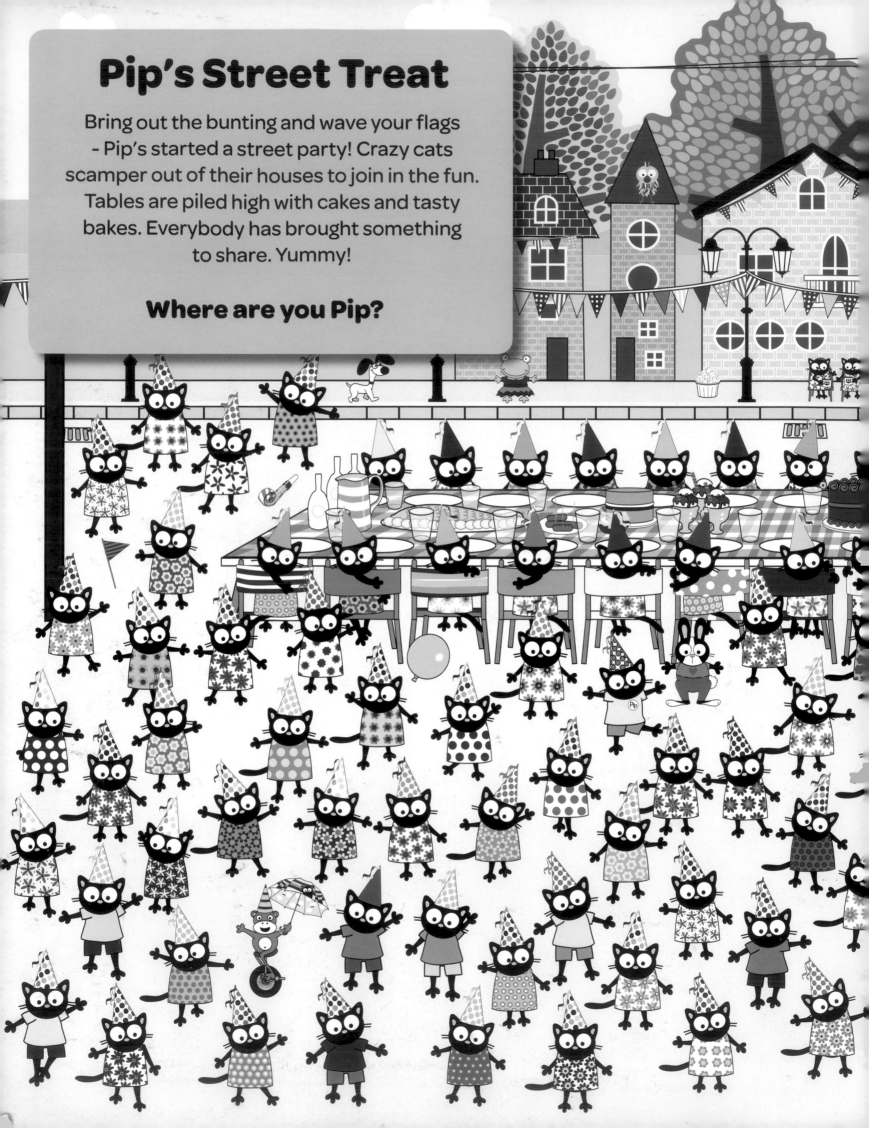

Pip's Street Treat

Bring out the bunting and wave your flags - Pip's started a street party! Crazy cats scamper out of their houses to join in the fun. Tables are piled high with cakes and tasty bakes. Everybody has brought something to share. Yummy!

Where are you Pip?

Pack up for Pip

Can you spot all of Pip's things?

Pip's Birthday Bash!

Hooray, hooray, it's Pip's birthday! The pussycat's pals have organized a very special surprise – a giant fancy dress party with cake, candles and games. Pip jives and jiggles on the dance floor. What a brilliant birthday bop!

Where are you Pip?

Happy Birthday Pip!

Pack up for Pip

Can you spot all of Pip's things?

Put Pip in the Picture

How did Pip get to be such a great dancer? The paw-footed puss has had lots of practice! Take a look back at the kitty's coolest party moves.

Pip shimmied at the sleepover.

The kitty whirled and twirled all around the ball.

All eyes were on Pip the prancing pirate.

Pip thrilled the Christmas party with a super skating sequence.

All the teddies were impressed at the woodland picnic!

Pip's swaying beach conga was far out!

At the spooky party, Pip made the guests gasp.

The garden gathering was the perfect time to flutter like a fairy.

The whole town turned out to watch Pip's sensational street moves!

Pip was the star of the dance floor at the birthday bash!

There's Pip!

Did you find Pip on every page? What a super hide-and-seeker. The little kitty loved playing this peeptastic party game. Give yourself a paw on the back!

Keep on seeking!

There are ten more things hiding in the pages of Pip's book. Can you find each and every one? Put a big tick next to every object that you spot.

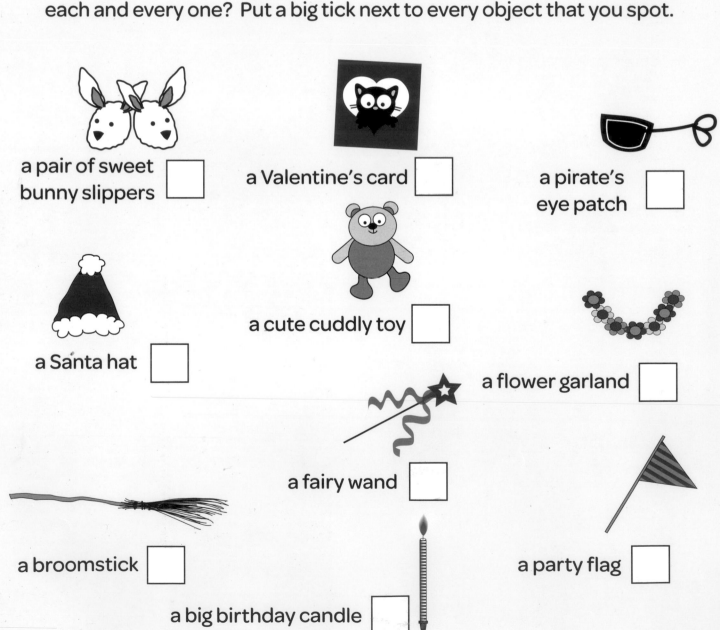

a pair of sweet bunny slippers ☐

a Valentine's card ☐

a pirate's eye patch ☐

a Santa hat ☐

a cute cuddly toy ☐

a flower garland ☐

a fairy wand ☐

a broomstick ☐

a big birthday candle ☐

a party flag ☐